# MONTEREY'S Adobe HERITAGE

PHOTOGRAPHY . . . . . . . . . WYNN BULLOCK

HISTORICAL OUTLINES . . . . . . MAYO HAYES O'DONNELL

DESIGN AND SKETCHES . . . . . . RUNYAN AND WHITMAN

EDITORIAL SUPERVISION . . . . . . . GASTON J. LEY

*Published and Presented as a Contribution to the*
*Preservation of Monterey's Historic Adobe Tradition by*
MONTEREY SAVINGS AND LOAN ASSOCIATION

Monterey's adobe heritage is an inspiring cultural treasure, a living relic of one of the most romantic eras in the history of our American Republic. In appreciation of the unique value of this heritage, our Association has undertaken the restoration of the Estrada Adobe, one of the finest examples of Early Monterey architecture.

It is with pleasure that we present this volume to all who share with us the feeling of pride in the possession of our splendid collection of California's finest historic monuments.

*Mary H. Mitchell*

President, Monterey Savings & Loan Association

1st Printing 1965 — 20,000 copies
2nd Printing 1968 — 10,000 copies

Copyright 1965 by Monterey Savings and Loan Association
Library of Congress Catalog Card Number: 64-8559

Lithographed in U. S. A. by W. T. Lee Printing Co., Monterey, California

The Monterey History and Art Association, Ltd. wishes hereby to give acclaim to the Monterey Savings and Loan Association which has been an inspiring and guiding force in the recognition of the need for preservation and enhancement of the beauty of this area and its historical landmarks, through the restoration of the Estrada Adobe, and in the development for present and future generations of an appreciation and enjoyment of the tradition inherent in Monterey.

❖

The Monterey History and Art Association, Ltd. salutes with gratitude the accomplishments of the Monterey Savings and Loan Association in the good taste so successfully expressed in combining the old and the new, in the modern building on Alvarado Street and the historic adobe, built in 1823, on Tyler Street, and in the landscaping which ties together the two buildings so successfully as one unit.

❖

The Monterey History and Art Association, Ltd. also gives acclaim to the Monterey Savings and Loan Association for its generosity in dedicating the use of a portion of the old and historic monument to the non-profit organizations on the Monterey Peninsula, as a gathering place.

❖

The resolution was passed and adopted at a meeting of the Board of Directors of the Monterey History and Art Association, Ltd. held in the Community Room of the Estrada Adobe on October 5, 1964.

The Monterey History and Art Association, Ltd.

# WHALING STATION

This fine old adobe, long known as the Old Whaling Station, faces on Decatur Street, near the Presidio entrance. It is a two story structure of charming simplicity which derives much of its distinctive character from a second-story balcony extending across the entire front.

The adobe was built in 1855 by David Wight, its first owner. Wight came to Monterey from Doddington, England, with his wife Isabel Marsh Wight, a native of Newcastle-on-Tyne.

The adobe home acquired its unusual name from the fact that it later became a boarding house for Portuguese whalers who made their headquarters at Monterey. A whalebone sidewalk is an unusual feature of the adobe.

A most attractive, well-kept garden, surrounded by a high wall of chalk rock, is located to the rear of the adobe. There seems to be no record of the origin of the old iron anchor situated under a large pepper tree in one corner of the garden.

# CASA AMESTI

Casa Amesti, on Polk Street near Alvarado, is probably one of the best examples of Monterey Colonial architecture in California. This two story adobe was built about 1825 by Don Jose Amesti, a Spanish Basque who came to Monterey on the "Panther" at the age of thirty. In 1824 he married Prudenciana Vallejo, the daughter of Don Jose Ignacio Vallejo.

Casa Amesti was later owned by Mrs. Frances Elkins, noted interior decorator. Mrs. Elkins died in 1953, willing the adobe to the National Trust for Historic Preservation.

Casa Amesti is now leased by the historic society to the Old Capital Club for use as a men's club.

# VASQUEZ ADOBE

This was originally a small one-story adobe on Dutra between Jefferson and Madison Streets. It has been added to, so that as it stands today, it bears little resemblance to the original building.

The Vasquez Adobe was the home of Dolores Vasquez, sister of the notorious bandit, Tiburcio Vasquez, who was born in Monterey in 1839. The adobe is situated just back of the old jail, from which Vasquez is said to have made several escapes.

Many years later, Louis W. Hill, son of the famous railroad builder, purchased the property and did the remodeling. The historic adobe is now owned by the City of Monterey and occupied by several city officials.

# CUSTOM HOUSE

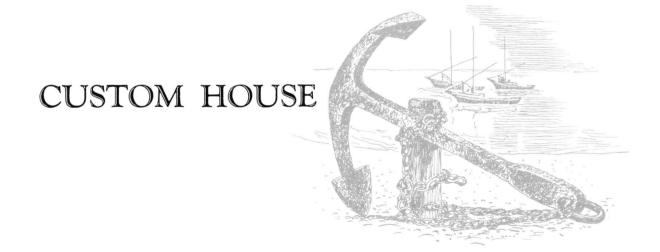

The Monterey Custom House Reservation is an outstanding historic site to which the State Division of Beaches and Parks obtained title from the Federal Government in 1930.

The site of the Custom House is the spot at which Commodore John Drake Sloat landed in 1846, raised the American Flag and took possession of California for the United States.

The Custom House was erected in 1814 during the Spanish period and added to under Mexican and American regimes. This famous old adobe symbolizes three periods in California history during each of which Monterey was Capital. It is now Number One State Historical Monument.

The Custom House is remarkably well preserved. From time to time it has been restored through the efforts of various community and state organizations. This building, with its exhibits of early California relics, has long been a shrine for students of history and other visitors to the Monterey Peninsula.

# MERRITT HOUSE

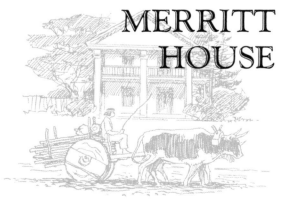

The Merritt House, a charming adobe residence on Pacific Street north of Franklin, was built by Don Ignacio Vallejo, who arrived in California from Mexico in 1774. In 1818, he is mentioned in connection with employment in certain public works in Monterey. Vallejo died in Monterey in 1831.

Josiah Merritt purchased the adobe in 1850. Merritt took an active part in organizing Monterey County and was at one time county judge.

Considerable improvement has been done on the property without destroying the old adobe atmosphere. It is in excellent state of preservation, with a charming formal garden facing Pacific Street.

# CASA ALVARADO

Casa Alvarado, on Dutra Street, was built in the early 1830's by Don Juan Bautista Alvarado, the first Monterey-born governor of California. He was the son of Don Jose Francisco Alvarado and Josefa Vallejo, and a direct descendant of Captain Cortez.

As was customary, the house was built to face east in order to take advantage of the morning sun at the front of the building. The twenty-four inch thick adobe walls are laid up with adobe mud as a mortar and supported on chalk rock foundations. Each room opens directly to the out-of-doors, a characteristic feature of the dwellings of this period.

# CASA BONIFACIO

One of the most famous homes in Monterey, built in 1835 on Alvarado Street at the corner of what is now known as Bonifacio Place, was that of Senorita Maria Ygnacia Bonifacio. In 1860 it became the home of Senora Pinto Bonifacio and passed on to her daughter Senorita Maria. Because of the legend of the planting of a rose by General William Tecumseh Sherman and the dainty senorita, the adobe became known as the Sherman Rose House.

In 1922, the adobe was taken down brick by brick and reconstructed in its original form on Mesa Road, where it stands today in all its beauty.

# HOUSE OF FOUR WINDS

"La Casa de los Vientos"—The House of Four Winds—was so called for the reason that it was the only building in early Monterey to have a weather vane on the roof. This adobe, located at 540 Calle Principal, was built about 1830.

The House of Four Winds was originally used as a residence, then as a store by Governor Alvarado, and later as the first hall of records in the State of California.

In 1914 this landmark was purchased and restored by the women of the Monterey Civic Club. A small auditorium was later added to the rear of the old building.

# COLTON HALL

When Commodore John Drake Sloat sailed into Monterey Bay and took possession of the old capital in 1846, the chaplain in the "Congress" was Walter D. Colton, to whom belongs the honor of erecting the first building of importance in California.

Colton Hall was started in 1847 and completed in March, 1849. In this building, from September 1 to October 15, 1849, assembled the constitutional convention under which California was admitted to statehood on September 9, 1850.

At that time it was said that Colton Hall was the finest and most pretentious building in all of California.

# CASA SANCHEZ

The Sanchez Adobe, located on the west side of Alvarado, between Franklin and Pearl Streets, is said to have been erected about 1829. It was a long, rambling one-story structure, with a veranda extending the full length at the rear and overlooking an elaborate garden which faced on Calle Principal. The Alvarado Street frontage extended to the southern wall of the portion now standing and embraced the present hardware store on the north.

The first record of ownership is credited to Gil Sanchez, who arrived from Mexico in 1820 and is reported to have been one of the founders of University of Santa Clara.

# STOKES ADOBE

The Stokes Adobe is one of the most distinguished old adobes of California's romantic period. It was built by Dr. James Stokes and is located on the southwest corner of Hartnell and Madison Streets.

Dr. Stokes was an English sailor who arrived in California in 1834 and married Josefa Soto in the same year. He later became a physician and was also Mayor of Monterey at one time.

It is said that much of the social life of the town centered in the Stokes Adobe, and its sala was famous for its social functions, including cascaron balls.

# CASA SERRANO

After Florencio Serrano courted and won the daughter of Don Joaquin de la Torre, he bought a piece of property on Calle Estrada (now Pacific Street) on which an adobe house had been started. Senorita de la Torre and Serrano were married in July, 1845 and made their home in the adobe which they completed. There Florencio had his school and there he died.

The Monterey History and Art Association some time ago purchased this historic adobe and has completely restored it as a permanent home for the organization. Since 1930, the Association has been collecting antique furniture and other historic items to place in the building.

# FIRST THEATRE

Jack Swan, a sailor, arrived in Monterey in 1843, and in the summer of the following year erected the adobe portion of the building now known as California's First Theatre. It is located at the corner of Scott and Pacific Streets. Swan used the building as a saloon and a sailors' boarding house for about two years.

In the fall of 1847, four army volunteers, here on military duty, joined by a small local group, gave two minstrel shows at Swan's Adobe and it became the first building on the Pacific Coast in which dramatic performances were staged. Later a group of men from Col. J. D. Stevenson's regiment of New York volunteers persuaded Swan to fit up the long wing for dramatic purposes.

The building is now a State Historic Monument and was re-opened as a theatre on June 3, 1937. Old-time melodramas are given there each week-end throughout the year.

# CASA
# de la TORRE

The de la Torre Adobe, built in 1852 by Francisco Pinto at Jefferson and Pierce Streets, facing the Friendly Plaza, is one of Monterey's charming old homes. It is a picturesque part of the altogether beautiful setting of Colton Hall, and with the Gordon House, Casa Alvarado, the Vasquez House and the Friendly Plaza, forms a part of the old Monterey which should always be kept intact and unspoiled by modernism.

Originally the home had only three rooms and an entrance hall, but from time to time, several lean-to's have been added. A lovely garden is at the front and rear.

# CASA de ORO

The Casa de Oro ("House of Gold"), at the corner of Scott and Olivier Streets, is said to have been erected before 1849 under orders from General Castro as a barracks for his men.

The origin of its name is uncertain. It is said to have at one time been a store, where gold dust was left for safe-keeping; a saloon, at which liquor was paid for in gold dust; and finally, a headquarters to which miners brought gold dust for exchange.

The building is now a State of California historic monument. The interior has been made into a replica of an old-time store.

ESTRADA ADOBE

The Estrada Adobe, on Tyler Street near Bonifacio Place, was erected by Don Jose Mariano Estrada for his residence about 1823. Early photographs show it as a two story building with balconies both front and rear.

By the 1880's the adobe had been converted into the three-storied St. Charles Hotel. In the early 1900's, it was again enlarged by the addition of a wing and became known as the Mission Inn.

The land on which the Mission Inn was located was purchased in 1961 by Monterey Savings and Loan Association to provide additional ground for the construction of a modern new Savings Center.

Because of the historic background of the Estrada Adobe, the Directors of Monterey Savings decided to restore the building to its original form, preserve it as a historic monument and dedicate it for community use.

# CASA
# JESUS SOTO

This old adobe on Pierce Street, erected by Francisco Soberanes, was sold to Jesus Soto to whom it was assessed in 1851 as "one adobe back of Colton Hall." The next owner was Manuel Soto who in turn sold it to Tony Dutra. From that time it was abandoned and for many years referred to as the "Bandit House."

Miss Josephine Blanch, an artist, purchased and restored the adobe in 1940, and sold it in 1944 to John Steinbeck, the famous author.

The charming old house is now owned by Dr. Harry Lusignan who maintains it as his office.

# FIRST FRENCH CONSULATE

The Girl Scout House on Lake El Estero was once the Consulate of France. Louis Gasquet, the first French Consul to California, occupied the house in 1845.

The historic old building originally stood on Fremont Street and Abrego and was popularly known as the "Tamale Parlor". In 1932 the Monterey History and Art Association took up the cause to save the old adobe from destruction. It was carefully taken apart and accurately reconstructed on its present site.

The old adobe occupied a real place in early California history and is of great historical value and architectural interest. It is now owned by the City of Monterey.

# CASA BORONDA

One of Monterey's earliest adobe residences is the Casa Boronda, built by Don Manuel de Boronda in 1817. This very fine old one story adobe occupies a delightfully secluded site on a knoll at the end of Boronda Lane.

Don Manuel de Boronda, a native of Spain, came to California as a corporal in the Spanish army during the early days of the Spanish Colonization movement. Boronda became a school teacher in San Francisco and continued his teaching after moving to Monterey.

Casa Boronda was one of the first adobe dwellings to be built outside the old Presidio wall.

# CASA GUTIERREZ

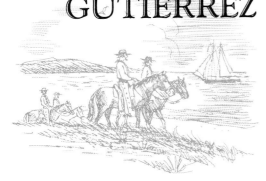

The Gutierrez Adobe, actually an adjoining pair of two-story buildings on Calle Principal near Madison, is believed to have been built by Nicolas Gutierrez, who served as Mexican governor of California in 1836.

In the early 1940's, the adobe was threatened with destruction to make way for a modern building. A group of interested citizens who made up the Monterey Foundation bought the building and preserved it as an example of Monterey architecture in the early Mexican period.

On June 29, 1954, the State of California was given title to the Casa Gutierrez—another link that binds Monterey to California's historic past.

# PACIFIC HOUSE

The Pacific House, at the intersection of Calle Principal and Alvarado Streets, is a long two-storied adobe building with a balcony on all four sides. It was built by James McKinley in 1835, originally as a hotel and saloon, the guests being principally sea-faring men. The entire grounds cover one-third of a modern city block.

In the early 1850's, McKinley sold the property to David Jacks, one of Monterey's prominent citizens. His daughter, Miss Margaret Jacks, later presented the building, with its former bull and bear pit arena grounds, to the State of California as a state historic monument.

The garden, located on the site of the old arena, is now known as "Memory Garden." It is enclosed by a high adobe wall and here the Monterey History and Art Association celebrates Monterey's birthday with a "Merienda" each June 3rd. The lower floor of the building is now a modern museum, open to the public.

# CASA BUELNA

In the very early days of Monterey the Presidio was located near El Estero and the Royal Presidio Chapel was within its walls. The inhabitants finally ventured outside the walls, almost within calling distance, to build their homes. Three such homes, located on the hills just to the south of Fremont Street, are Casa Buelna, Casa de Castro and Casa Boronda.

Casa Buelna was built by Antonio Buelna, Mexican soldier turned school teacher, during the years 1818-1821. He established in the adobe a girls' school which was later operated by Senora Hillaria de Buelna.

A large section of the grounds surrounding Casa Buelna has been developed into a magnificent garden.

# FIRST BRICK HOUSE

The first brick house in California still stands on Decatur Street, between Pacific and Alvarado Streets. It was built by order of Gallant Duncan Dickinson of Virginia. Dickinson and family came to California with the Donner Party which started in 1846 from Independence, Missouri.

On May 31, 1848, Dickinson bought the land on Decatur Street for twenty-nine dollars. The work on the brick house was done by Dickinson's son-in-law, a brick mason, who molded, fired and laid the brick.

The house contains three rooms on each floor. Dickinson had planned a larger house, but one of the wings was never constructed.

CASA SOBERANES

Casa Soberanes, on Pacific Street, sometimes known as "The House with the Blue Gate," was built about 1830 by Don Jose Estrada, ranking officer of the Presidio of Monterey under Mexican rule. Estrada sold the property to Don Feliciano Soberanes, who married one of the daughters of Don Ignacio Vallejo. In 1902 the adobe was purchased by Jean Booth Serrano and her husband, Reuban L. Serrano, a grandson of the former alcalde of Monterey under Mexican rule.

The property again changed ownership in 1941, when it was acquired by Mr. and Mrs. William O'Donnell. On June 3, 1953, Mrs. O'Donnell presented the historic adobe to the State of California to become an Historic Monument, retaining for herself a life interest in the property.

The "sala", or drawing room of this home has been used as an example of early American adobe in the Chicago Art Museum's Thorne collection of miniature rooms.

# CARMEL MISSION

This beautiful mission of San Carlos de Borromeo del Carmelo was founded in June, 1771, on the Carmel River. Both the river and the mission were named in honor of the Carmelite Fathers.

The present building was begun in 1793 and dedicated in September, 1797. Being beautifully situated and prosperous, it became the headquarters for the Father Presidents of all the missions in California.

Elevation of Carmel Mission to the rank of Basilica in 1960 places it in a highly dignified position. This rank has been conferred on only eleven other churches in the United States.

# ROYAL PRESIDIO CHAPEL

This chapel, located in the old Presidio, is the only remaining part of the Church of San Carlos de Borromeo de Monterey, which had its birth on June 3, 1770, when Father Junipero Serra and Don Gaspar de Portola met at Monterey to establish the church and claim California for Mexico.

A fire in 1789 damaged the church beyond repair. Workmen from Mexico built a new church which was dedicated in 1795. Among these workmen was a stone carver, Manuel Ruiz, who is thought to have carved the figure of the Patron Saint of Mexico, "The Virgin of Guadalupe", high atop the front facade.

# GORDON HOUSE

The Gordon House, located at the corner of King and Pierce Streets, is one of the most charming of the old wooden houses in Monterey. Lumber for the Gordon House was milled in Australia, shipped to England, and reshipped around the Horn to Monterey.

A plain frame house, it was built in 1849-50 by Phillip Roach, last alcalde and first mayor of Monterey. One of the first all-wooden houses to be built in California, its design follows the simple lines and pattern of the adobes.

In 1871, Samuel B. Gordon, from whom the house at present takes its name, became the owner.

# FIRST FEDERAL COURT

Don Jose de la Torre, a Mexican alcalde, built this charming adobe on the corner of Hartnell and Polk Streets about 1832. Here he held the first Federal Court in 1836 under Mexican rule and was still holding court in the adobe when Americans took possession of California in 1846.

The whole building is hand-fashioned. Many of its window panes are of handmade glass, brought around the Horn from New England.

The First Federal Court Adobe is a good example of preservation for use of one of the oldest buildings in Monterey. It is now owned by the Hudson family and serves as Tom Hudson's law offices.

# CAPITULAR HALL

Still standing on the corner of Pacific and Franklin Streets is the two-story house erected in 1834 by Guy Freeman Fling of Sonora, Upper California. Originally the adobe was a one-story house, but a second story frame addition was added many years ago.

In the early days the building was always known as "Capitular Hall", which leads us to believe that it was the town hall of the day.

Fling sold the property to John Donelly, a teamster of the U. S. Artillery, on June 28, 1848. On August 18th of the same year, the property was purchased by Thomas Oliver Larkin. Consideration was three ounces in gold—uncoined.

# CASA ABREGO

Casa Abrego, at Abrego and Webster Streets, is one of the oldest landmarks in Monterey. The home was built by Don Jose Abrego, a Spanish merchant who came to Monterey from Mexico in 1834 on the vessel "La Natalie", the ship on which Napoleon is said to have escaped from the Isle of Elba.

One night the ship drifted ashore in a storm and was wrecked. Timbers from the historic ship were used by Don Abrego in the construction of his home.

Casa Abrego was purchased in 1956 by a group of women and is now the home of the Casa Abrego Club for Women.

# CASA PACHECO

Casa Pacheco, on the southwest corner of Abrego and Webster Streets, was built in 1840 by Don Francisco Pacheco, who came from Mexico in 1819 as sub-lieutenant of the Mexican artillery. Pacheco became one of the wealthiest landowners in the county.

The two-story adobe originally had a main entrance on Webster Street, by way of a large recessed veranda, with a gallery of considerable dimensions above. Small wrought iron balconies adorned the windows facing the two streets. The roof was tiled and the rooms large and square.

Casa Pacheco is now a luncheon and social club for men, owned by the membership of the club.

# STEVENSON HOUSE

The Stevenson House is located on Houston Street, formerly known as Merchant's Row, between Pearl and Webster Streets. The original owner was Don Rafael Gonzales. This fine old two-story adobe, at one time known as the French Hotel, was renamed in honor of Robert Louis Stevenson, who lived for several months at the hotel while visiting Monterey in 1879.

The building is now a State of California historical monument. The lower floor is a repository for much Stevensoniana, while a house museum occupies the second floor. Much of the Stevenson material came from Stevenson's stepdaughter, the late Mrs. Isobel Field.

# CASA JOAQUIN SOTO

The Joaquin Soto Adobe enjoys a secluded setting at the end of Via Joaquin, a short lane off of Eldorado Street. Litigation regarding the property began over one hundred years ago when Joaquin died at the age of ninety-seven and left a will written in Spanish. The original file showing the petition of probate of the will is still preserved in the office of the Monterey County Clerk.

The property later became the home of Augustin Soto, grandson of Joaquin. Augustin lived in the adobe till his death in 1942, when it was purchased and restored by Mrs. Mary L. Greene. Although Mrs. Greene added two adobe brick rooms, the character of the home was well retained. All the original roof tile was set back in place and care was taken to preserve the exterior woodwork.

The Joaquin Soto Adobe now serves as the medical offices of its present owner, Dr. Scott Heath. It is an excellent example of the adaptation of an historic adobe to modern use.

# GENERAL FREMONT HEADQUARTERS

This small two-story adobe building on Hartnell Street, long known as the headquarters of General John Charles Fremont, was saved from destruction through purchase by the Monterey History and Art Association. General Fremont was in Monterey County during 1846 and 1847, so it is quite possible that the adobe could have been his military headquarters during his stay here.

A 115 year old map of the City of Monterey shows the existence of a building on the present site of this Fremont Adobe. The ancient Narvaez map is carefully stored away in the office of the city tax collector. The building is presently occupied by the Monterey Peninsula Board of Realtors.

# CASA
## de CASTRO

The Castro Adobe, on Castro Road facing the Del Monte Fairways, was originally the summer home of General Jose Castro and his family. General Castro was born in Monterey, where he served as secretary of the Common Council, Prefect of the Monterey District and Commandant of the Department of the North under Spanish rule.

The Castro Adobe was purchased a number of years ago by the late Miss Margaret Jacks, who restored the structure and made it her home for many years. At present, under new ownership, both the exterior and interior of the adobe present a perfect picture of true early California hospitality.

# COOPER-MOLERA ADOBE

The Cooper-Molera Adobe, on the southwest corner of Polk and Munras, is one of the largest of the Monterey adobes. A two-story balconied structure, it has been well preserved and today is still owned by a descendant of the original builder.

The adobe was built by Juan Bautista Cooper, a native of Alderney Island in the British Channel. He was a half-brother of Thomas Oliver Larkin, first and only American Consul to Monterey. Cooper came to Monterey in 1826, having arrived in California as the master of his own ship, "The Rover".

Cooper married Dona Encarnacion Vallejo, a sister of General Vallejo.

# SHERMAN HEADQUARTERS

Next to the Larkin House on Calle Principal is an attractive small adobe built in 1834 by Thomas Oliver Larkin. From 1847 to 1849 it was the quarters of Lieutenant William T. Sherman, who later became the famous general, and General Henry W. Halleck, Secretary of State after the Mexican occupation.

In his Memoirs, General Sherman writes of this as the little adobe back of Larkin's. This is explained by the fact that the Larkin House at that time faced Jefferson Street.

General Sherman (then lieutenant) arrived in Monterey in 1847 on the "California", the first Pacific Mail steamship to reach the territory.

LARKIN HOUSE

Monterey's historic Larkin House, on Calle Principal, was presented to the State of California as an historic monument on March 16, 1957 by Larkin's grand-daughter, Mrs. Alice Larkin Toulmin.

The 120 year old structure is distinguished as one of the earliest examples of Monterey architecture. It was named the Thomas Oliver Larkin State Historical Monument as a tribute to the memory of California's first and only American Consul.

The Larkin House was built in 1834, shortly after Larkin came to California as a Yankee merchant. He was appointed U. S. Consul to California in 1843. From then until 1848 his house was the consulate and much of the time filled with visitors.

Larkin House contained the office of Walter Colton, first American alcalde of Monterey, and later served as headquarters for the U. S. Military Governor of California. The home is open to the public five days each week.

# UNDERWOOD-BROWN ADOBE

The Underwood-Brown Adobe, at the south end of Friendly Plaza facing Pacific Street, is now incorporated into the Few Memorial Building and serves as the City Manager's office.

The older portion of the building was erected by Santiago Stokes, who sold the property to Jose Maria Sanchez in 1843. The deed describes how the new owner opened and closed doors, pounded on walls and scattered handfuls of dirt on the back yard as rituals of ownership.

In 1866 the property was sold to Charles Underwood for $650 and was in the possession of the Underwood family until it became city owned.

# CASA MADARIAGA

An attractive little Mexican adobe home on Abrego Street opposite Casa Pacheco later came to be known as Casa Madariaga.

Juan Madariaga married a widow who had acquired title to Rancho Pescadero through her husband's death.

Maria did not enjoy ranch life. She wished for life in the social whirl of the old capital—"a good adobe casa in Monterey where from between shuttered windows a woman could look out on life and romance."

In 1846 Maria got her wish. She sold her rancho—more than 4000 good acres—for $500 and purchased a house in town. The house is now known as the Madariaga Adobe.

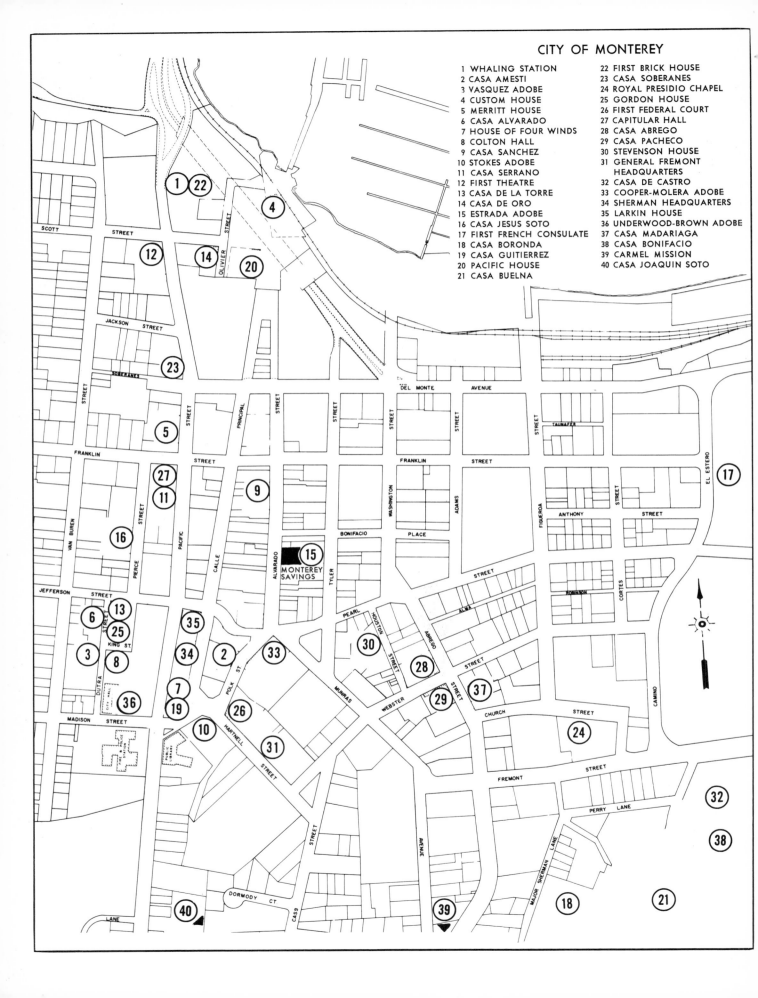

# CITY OF MONTEREY

1 WHALING STATION
2 CASA AMESTI
3 VASQUEZ ADOBE
4 CUSTOM HOUSE
5 MERRITT HOUSE
6 CASA ALVARADO
7 HOUSE OF FOUR WINDS
8 COLTON HALL
9 CASA SANCHEZ
10 STOKES ADOBE
11 CASA SERRANO
12 FIRST THEATRE
13 CASA DE LA TORRE
14 CASA DE ORO
15 ESTRADA ADOBE
16 CASA JESUS SOTO
17 FIRST FRENCH CONSULATE
18 CASA BORONDA
19 CASA GUITIERREZ
20 PACIFIC HOUSE
21 CASA BUELNA

22 FIRST BRICK HOUSE
23 CASA SOBERANES
24 ROYAL PRESIDIO CHAPEL
25 GORDON HOUSE
26 FIRST FEDERAL COURT
27 CAPITULAR HALL
28 CASA ABREGO
29 CASA PACHECO
30 STEVENSON HOUSE
31 GENERAL FREMONT
   HEADQUARTERS
32 CASA DE CASTRO
33 COOPER-MOLERA ADOBE
34 SHERMAN HEADQUARTERS
35 LARKIN HOUSE
36 UNDERWOOD-BROWN ADOBE
37 CASA MADARIAGA
38 CASA BONIFACIO
39 CARMEL MISSION
40 CASA JOAQUIN SOTO